—With a song and a prayer from the Rubio!

Herb Brin

Apr. 22, '96

POEMS from the RUBIO

Herb Brin

POEMS from the RUBIO

Herb Brin

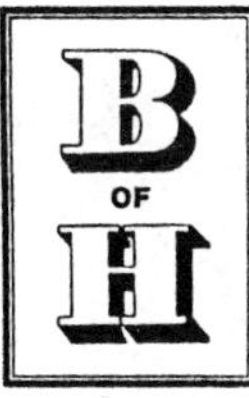

BOOKS OF HERITAGE
A DIVISION OF
HERITAGE PUBLISHING COMPANY
2130 S. Vermont Ave., Los Angeles, CA 90007
Tel: (213) 737-2122

POEMS FROM THE RUBIO

Address all inquiries to:

Books of Heritage
2130 S. Vermont Avenue
Los Angeles, California 90007

Library of Congress
Catalog Card Number: 95-75701

1. Regional poetry, (California).
2. Jewish Religious Poetry, American.
ISBN: 0-9645651-0-2

Printed in the United States of America

DEDICATION

For those especially
to whom I sing:
thoughtful Miriam of rare concerns
sparkling Sarah of winsome eye
Nathan of my childhood dreams
and Ben the charmer of ideas
and those who follow as I sing
for Ariana, gentle Ariana
And for you!

Aug 18, 93

ELIE WIESEL

My dear Hess —

Your melancholy poems, filled with melody and light, are beautiful —

How a journalist, how an editor could also be a brilliant poet, is to me a source of astonishment. And of gratitude —

Shana tova to you and your family —

Your friend:

Elie

"The hoary head is a crown of glory."

— Proverbs 16:31

As an editor and poet, Herb Brin has developed a vision that spans many continents, many landscapes, many eras. Among his tasks has been the redemption of Jewish voices that have been drowned by history — a redemption wrought by poems that express these martyrs' agonies and yearnings with immediacy and passion. Not surprisingly, in this volume, too, Herb is a traveler, witnessing for the slain and the silence in Dubrovnik, Munich, Paris, Hong Kong.

More tellingly, however, Herb has at last come home, home to the Rubio, his canyon-surrounded mountaintop in California, where "all is remembrance," home to nature and the "relentless, remorseless" instinct "to live another day," home to his body, to the "remembrance of a first kiss" while a nurse's aide preps him for heart surgery, home to "my father's house" where "eternity is brittle" and yet "prayers still ascends in mystic ways . . ."

"How goodly are thy tents, O Jacob, thy dwellings, O Israel!" And how good to come home with you, Herb! Even during the blackout atop the Rubio, your light shines; even anesthetized and ready for the scalpel, your heart beats strong and warm.

Alexander M. Schindler

By Way of Commentary

Despite the darknesses that have engulfed Jewish people over the centuries — and the darknesses were real and bitter — this extraordinary people managed to sing. The more terrible the event, the more fervent the song.

As Jews were being marched into the German camps of death, they sang *Ani Maamin.* "I believe with perfect faith in the coming of the Messiah."

They may take the lives of our people, our children, our patriarchs; they may not take our Jewish song.

Our accents may be in Aramaic or in Hebrew, in Ladino or in Yiddish. Or in the only language that I know, English. But our rhythm patterns — our Jewish genes! — project the happy but always melancholy Jewish song.

Beat a rhythm on your chest while humming George Gershwin's *Summertime,* slowly, and you encounter the cantorial chant.

Jewish song transcended Torquemada, Bogdan Chmielnicki (Chmiel the wicked!), the Czar of Russia, Hitler. The Jewish song, in the *extremis* of a people, is now forever part of German memory, Spanish memory, Russian memory — never in history to be separated. The Jewish song remains inviolate. The eternal Jewish song. *Kol Nidré.* Therefore I sing.

I have asked four friends for commentary on these *Poems from the Rubio:* Prof. Elie Wiesel, the poet of the

Holocaust and Nobel Laureate; Dr. Alexander Schindler, president of the Union of American Hebrew Congregations; Dr. Peter Gimpel, a classic scholar in Latin and Greek poetics, now a Lubavitch *Chassid;* and Jacob Pressman, Conservative rabbi and poet of remarkable depth.

Such commentary is necessary because poetic scholarship in the nation is often limited to games of literary back-scratching, games the serious poet must refuse to play. And if the poet is serious, he must be heard.

At this point I hasten to explain that the Rubio is a large canyon in the rugged San Gabriel Mountains reaching from the Rose Bowl to Mount Wilson. I live in a tiny home on a shoulder of the Rubio, where I do my writing.

The home was spared from the great fires which in October of 1993 destroyed the beautiful brush and forests of the Rubio. The fires halted inches from the home. The deer and the songbirds fled. The crickets fled. The coyotes fled. I was left in utter loneliness.

By Way of Gratitude

It is necessary to extend my gratitude to those at HERITAGE Publications for their help in the production of this fifth volume of my poetry, especially to Rabbi William Kramer, who has encouraged a peripatetic journalist into fields of song that might seem audacious to many. Especially to me.

Dan Brin, editor of HERITAGE, my son and my assignment editor, has gone over the material with savage intensity but with heart, and an earnest awareness of the overtones of these poems. My son, my friend.

Robert Lupo, who has taken a leap of faith beyond UCLA sports and the poetry of rhyme, which he loves so much, has brought home to me the essential truth that the poem must communicate or the poet must perish to other fields.

My gratitude to Hector Antichi, graphic artist for HERITAGE Publications, who designed the book in all its elements, the first volume to have the Books of HERITAGE imprimatur.

Barrie Beckman, chief typesetter for HERITAGE Publications, selected the Garamond typefaces used in the text with great care for his own artistic requirements.

The David Rose cover for the book reflects the artistry which has carried Rose to the forefront of courtroom artists in the nation.

Bertha Bernstein, as office manager of HERITAGE for

four decades, made possible our entry into the field of book publication, and Stan Boruck, who divides proof-reading chores with a penchant for film acting, is credited with assuring the inviolability of spelling correctness.

And beautiful Ann Siegel added her own poetic grace to the paste-up process. For art always graces the artist.

Peace and quietude have returned to the devastated Rubio and my neighbor, the Rev Elizabeth Davenport, reports that she has seen two young deer scanning the roses in my garden, from afar. Beautiful, beautiful Elizabeth! She gave them the roses.

And the coyotes are back. And bluebirds are on the wing. Again. Life is indeed beautiful on our Rubio.

Pray for rain.

Herb Brin

CONTENTS

CONTENTS

Yesterday's Garden

In My Father's House

My Father's house is a spaceship
In the sky
A planet of immensity that seeks
Its magnet paths from dawn
To dawn to dawn
One day to die.

In my Father's house
The orders have been set
The microbes and the hungers
And the angers
And the sighs
The seasons in their time
The laughter
And the sweet bitterness of being.

In my Father's house
Birds must leave their nests
And seeds are sown for harvests
Or desires
And babies cry to seek
The narrowing breasts
As clouds collide to stir
Awakening storms.

In my Father's house
They mastered arts of fire
How to romance fields
And flowers
And comprehend the spectra
And the hours.

In my Father's house
They studied pathways of the thunder winds
Lashed to plunderships
Upon forbidden seas
While warlords point their madness
To cindered ecstasies
As streams run toxic
In an alchemy of tears
And dreams are stolen
Ravaged and debased
Where theft is king.

In my Father's house
Prayers still ascend in mystic ways
To slow the whirling spaceship
In the sky
As I unleash what Prometheus hardly knew:
Reflections that eternity is brittle
In my Father's house
And I have done these things
All these things
In my Father's house.

April 17, 1985
Santa Monica

Firestorm Over Shasta

Trees are cathedral, templar
Through forests of the redwood
Giants of the earth, awesome in remembrance
Of idyllic days and fire nights
Of the great species that roamed the brush
And expired to storms and new concerns
Of the selection process
Which decrees, which forever decrees
Who may live and who may not
In the cathedral shadows, the redwood shadows
The awesome prayer halls of survival.

The walls of forest restrain me
To my Sable
Carefully to my Sable, cautioned by a sign:
"Deer crossing ahead"
And I wonder: Who would harm a deer
In the redwoods toward Eureka?

Eureka!
I found the coastal city an assumption
Of Victorian pose
And closed banks
And plastic antiques
Beside the Samoa Cookhouse
Where logging butchers
Paused for gastronomic momentries
On other days ago.

Eureka!
Now largely a domain

Of bedlam hostelries
Which abound the roadway
Squeezing hot nickels and sweaty dimes
From wanderers of the way
Who flee Eureka, having found it
The lumpy beds befouled
With incensed memories of India past.

Eastward to the Trinity
And beyond
Where fires encase the Shasta
While waters, unquenching waters,
    slam their way
Through still primeval forests

Soon to be decapitated in chainsaw whim
Whee!
Or by flame.

To Whiskeytown, again
Where once, ago, ago
I invented time
But not now to raise a glass
In Whiskeytown
Nor pause to take a cognac
At Brandy Creek
(Or whatever else it's called)
Where the rich of Shasta look skyward,
Apprehensive of the dark clouds
That shadow trees surrounding Whiskeytown
Where tiny boats now moor
Ominous under fire clouds of summer.

Oh, forget the fiery skies.
In this idyll of the redwoods
Long memories away from '49
Where parents came from Red Bluff
With their child
Now encased in hallowed ground
Beside a highway Trinity.

Drive gently as you pass the grave
Of the pioneer Jewish baby
    east of Whiskeytown.

Clouds gather fearsome over Shasta
And all the way to Calaveras
Where frogs leaped for Twain
Memories ago
Beyond the mournful Trinity
Now white of the boiling waters
That carve imprints of eternity
On boulder banks
Without concern for the black clouds
That consume their way
Through forests to the sea.

A fawn crossed my pathway
And watching him I mused:
Will sorrows and suffocation,
The constants of the forest
Be far behind?

Aug. 30, 1992
On the Rubio

Atop the Rubio

Gone are the songbirds
And the song from my trees
On the mountain atop the Rubio.

The pines are shedding needles
In disarray, forming blankets of thorn
To warm the roots,
Impending storms are chilling
As the life cycles have it.

I am left with crickets in the night
The unrelenting sound of endless,
 melancholy rasps
From all the shadows of the night
With only a sliver moon to comfort me
In the awesomeness of darks on darks
And a cacophony of sound
Portending the arrival of autumn's winds
In the stark lonesomeness of gusts
Whispering through the brush.

Soon the rains will come
And life exists in burrows on the mountain
While in my tiny home
Nestling on the Rubio
I kindle logs to warm the hearth
And abuse the chill
Of the new season's wintry will.

No longer is the eternal test:
When winter comes, for me,

How far beyond is spring?

The control of life cycles
Has not been given me nor thee
If winter comes
When winter comes.

On the Rubio are no forevers
But on the mountain, too, there will be spring
And the beautiful deer, the gentle deer
Will race the butterflies
For the wildflowers and the berries
Dancing colors against a cloudless sky.

And the songbirds will return
To enchant the shadows
And if I am there -- oh, if I am there
I will sing with them, again
And sigh.

Oct. 7, 1991
On the Rubio

The Rubio Is Mine

On loan, as life itself is on loan
In the savage wilderness of being,
The Rubio is mine.

Cascading canyons surround me
While songbirds dance among the wildflowers
That embrace me
In the shadows of oak and pine
That genuflect in the wind
To the mountain tops
And beyond, beyond
To the eternity of the blue called the sky.

Here all is remembrance
Or nothing at all.

June 30, 1993
On the Rubio

In My Forest

When it rains, as it must
And the day darkens
As it does for my friends of the forest
And the voice of the cricket is still
On the mountainside
Where the mockingbird seeks refuge
In the silence of the rain
And the graceful deer
The beautiful, the swift deer
Huddle in the brush

As the sanctuary of night
Becomes the miracle of life extension
For my forest friends
And the species are temporarily safe
One from the other until the dawn
When clouds begin to part again
Over my mountain
And a rooster crows across the Rubio
A bird sings, and then another
While the apprehensive deer venture softly
Into my garden in the cloud.

There go the roses which I tend
With tenderness
The rosebuds of my garden

In the dim, fragrant light they disappear
Flower by flower
Petal by petal of many colors
Of many fragrances they disappear
To the deer upon my mountain
Who do not know of beauty
Only hungers, in my forest.

June 4, 1989
On the Rubio

Life's Cycle

As the carousel of cloud in orbit
Turns round and round and round
Somewhere turns the worm
Where gophers burrow
To the roots of being.

The sun winks an eye
Of fire from the sky
With a nod to the moon
And the stars
In a time called night.

In the darkened forest
Rattles chatter imponderables
As slithering halts
And all is apprehension
For life's moment
Fearsome
Wrapped in silence for the predator
As wildcat and coyote
Stalk their prey for survival
In the silenced dark.

Overhead the bluebird
Leaves its perch atop the pine
And flies a graceful arch
Swift in the early light
And of a sudden, swoops

Attacks the mountainside
To grasp a turning worm
In life's cycle
Relentless, remorseless
To live another day.

July 14, 1989
On the Rubio

A Single Cry

In the mountains of the Rubio
The ground hogs (or however
  they are known here)
Are yet to see their shadows
Portending winter's end.

Soon, as it is said.

In the quietudes of desert
Half the world away
Missiles are very pointed, pointed, pointed
At my heart.

Why am I here
In the mountains of the Rubio
As Scuds slam furies
Upon my memories
And sirens beckon children
To be brave
While some must grieve on battlements
In Tel Aviv
In sealed rooms to hold away the fumes
Targeted by Babylon
Once charted in Berlin.

In the darknesses of night
My TV tube clicks aside its CNN convulsions
And in the lonesome shadows of the dark

My Rubio canyon shudders
And it seems I hear a scream
The voice so young, a single cry: "Help me!"

And then no more
As half a world away the guns go on with war.

Feb. 8, 1991
On the Rubio

Darkness on the Rubio

And then, of course, the lights went out
In my mountain home
As they must in one's mountain home
Upon the Rubio.

Mountain home?
Oh, there are oaks in abundance
And pine, and brush all about.
Today the last songbird of the season
Called on me in kindness
And the gurgling blackbirds
Are now in dominance in the skies
For the emerging winter season.

But a mountain home in darkness on the Rubio?
How terrible to contemplate the dark
Without cable CNN
Or the hum of refrigerator.

The full moon smiles
To slither beams through pines about me
Protecting the Rubio
From hot desert winds.

In the silences
Even the crickets are awed
By the unelectrified dark
And the owls are silent
And the coyotes, in the eeriness
Of the uncanny shadows
And the electrified radio

Is silent on the Rubio
Where we conclude our covenant
With the essential state
Call it reality, the state of being
In the dark.

But there must be a way
Man in his ardor
Called by grace as wisdom
Must stumble along, assembling thoughts
For eternity
Even in the dark.

And in darkening shadows
I stumble to the stairwell
To count the steps
They are 12, down to the kitchen
And its ledge where once upon a memory
I had placed a candleholder
Brought from a visit to Riad El Bahia
Hotel, somewhere in the world
With a candle in place
For one day on the Rubio
When darkness would engulf
 my mountain home.

But disaster loomed without a match
A mountain home without a match
As the moon in satire

Smiles cautiously through the slithers
Of beam which are insistent
That when man walked the moon,
Abusing eternal stillness on the moon
It wasn't I!

Oh, given time in the recesses
Of the human engine
The lights returned to my mountain home
Upon the Rubio
And before the dawn the owls will hoot
Their eeriness
And somewhere a coyote will raise
    its snout to the moon
And howl.

Then in contemplation:
If the poet were blind
As often poets are
How to test for values on the Rubio
In the dark
How to test for wisdom
In a song?

Nov. 16, 1992
On the Rubio
In the dark

A Rubio Lullaby

A yellow iridescence
Oh, not golden, not golden
My moon over the Rubio is mystic yellow
Now a cradle of fire source
At night, on its back
A moon-cradle halted in midrock
Once tamed by footsteps of leaping giants.

My moon over the Rubio
Weaves mystic patterns for me
In the mountain shadows
Where I am tempted to sing
A long forgotten melody
Of sighs, of many sighs ago:
Lu-li lu-li-lu
Lu-li lu-li-lu
Pink of cheek and blue of eye
Oh long ago my baby cried
Mother sang a tender tune
Of almonds on the moon.

My tears are far away and bitter
For in the shadows of the Rubio
Beneath a yellow cradle in the sky
I alone remember.

June 30, 1993
On the Rubio

An Owl on the Rubio

Fires ring the Rubio above the Rose Bowl
And an owl of fearsome sound
Has found my forest
Where crickets cry their sorrows
Their unrelenting sorrows
That now enflame the canyons
    of the mountains.

Such sounds are always ominous
On the Rubio
Where spent grass, now crisp now vulnerable
Awaits the slash of flame racing wildly
Before a whoosh of winds
That carpet the canyons with disaster.

Where will my mountain animals go
The deer, the tender gentle deer
And the songbirds will find no home
Upon the Rubio.

But now an owl of fearsome fear
Driven by the storm of fire
Has come to my trees
Seeking comfort on my Rubio.
I sigh in welcome to my unseen friend
For as he fares, my home will fare
On our Rubio.

Aug 15, 1992
On the Rubio

I Hear the Bluebird Cry

In the dull morning of the mountains
The swift highway to Banff
Is silent beneath the tires
Of my LeBaron.

Of a sudden the sun explodes
And the summer rain
Paints enchantments
Of the essential colors
And shamelessly I sing a childhood song
Alone in my LeBaron
As a rainbow sharpens an eyebrow arch
Above a traffic-yellowed ice cap
Where the sky is blue
Ice blue.

Enthralled, I search for bluebirds
Which always fly, do they not
Higher even than the ice fields of Banff.

But I really find no bluebirds
Nor pots of gold
In this rainbow reverie
Seeking sources of my bedazzlement.

Somewhere over the rainbow
And the colors follow me
Along an undulating river of highway
Amidst these glaciers of Alberta

Where I embrace the mysteries
Of long forgotten melodies.

A scraggly mountain squirrel
Leaps out across the roadway
Then is halted by indecision
As I screech the brakes of my LeBaron
To spare the tiny animal
Which then flies against the wheel
Of an oncoming car
Selecting another to be the killer.

Life, as it must, ebbs
For frightened animal
Now making circles in the roadway dust,

Its body hurtled into concentrics
By the impact
As traffic races on.

Across the icefields is still the rainbow
Arching above the glaciers
Of forever.
But now I hear no childhood singing
Over this rainbow
Nor does the bluebird fly, this day
Over the mountains to Banff.

Yet it seems, in softest tone
I hear the bluebird cry.

August 31, 1989
Coeur D'Alene, Idaho

Reflections from a Gurney

Given time, an entity loses identity.

Profundities race the mind
Vapid, aboard a gurney
To the cutting room
Surprising how shallow are the profundities
And all is illusion aboard a gurney
To the cutting room.

The mind is a tyrant aboard my gurney:
Where is rage
I have need for rage in my waning years.

Shadows of the twisted cross surround me
And even now the silences of Rome
Are merciless and hot, taunts of fire
That I found as a child of the century
One gifted with song
With leaden song, and sorrows.

Upon the pathways of this gurney
Only the fragile and the mundane may enter:
Wake at four
To a clogged freeway in the early dawn
Arriving late at Saint John's
But soon enough, soon enough.

A ground war rages in the distant sands
Will I awake to learn its outcome?
Will I awake, indeed?
No matter
Tyranny forever jockeys for the rails

And nations for control in these things
While generals assuming power
Decree who shall live and who shall not
Governance by men playing games.

Nurses race to have me ready
For the alternatives
Shaving of groin hair to raise embarrassments
Remembrances of a first kiss
A sweet, stolen sigh
As sensation still tingles when the young
Attractive aide poses disinterest and distance
As she handles genitalia with composure.

Once such tenderness would earn its own reward
But then, how did that song go?
Once I built a railroad
And perhaps now aboard my gurney
Perhaps it's done
Sister, can you spare a sigh?

Pressures on my arm
Needles for the tubes of sustenance
A nun takes my hand
No time to ask my faith and suddenly
Her Lord's Prayer hovers over me
As quixotically I try to explain:
"You've got the wrong guy -- I am a Jew!"
But she squeezes my hand
Heart surgery is serious business
Her eyes closed in prayer

So I take my blessing as I can
Winking at her crucifix
For how is she to know *(Sh'ma Yisroel)*
That they are reciting prayers for me
At my synagogue, and even in Jerusalem
Where faith began.

Another nurse races to my gurney
With documents which I cannot read
But for God's sake I must sign
Before the curtain rises
To a laser exploration of arteries
Of many, many years.

By the living powers vested in me
By the semen of my father
Long, long gone
I approve, I approve open heart surgery
Should it come to that
But with a sudden horrifying thought
Should I not survive
And in some unattended recess of man's madness
I'll not be there to break the arm
Of Hitler (as I must, forever must!)
My sobbing will be forever.
Even in the eternities
There may be no surrender
No victories, again, for evil.

The valium is large and white and gentle
As I write
Thoughts wander to the deer on my mountain

My parched mountain in this arid year
My beautiful, my gentle, my famished deer.

I call out: "Sister, Sister, pray with me for rain..."
That the grasses will return
To my mountain
For a mountain may not be devoid of deer.

I put aside these thoughts
My gurney moves
Eternity does not hurt forever.

Feb. 22, 1991
Santa Monica

Unter den Linden

I saw a changing of the guard
Unter den Linden
Tall men, bearing guns, presenting arms
Nordic men
About face, stiff, deliberate
Automatons, raising legs
Goosestep Unter den Linden
Again.

It seems I saw a multitude
Unter den Linden
A master race, men, women
Screaming, chanting beaming euphoria
Tomorrow will be theirs
And the tomorrows of tomorrow.

The Yellow Star upon the breast
It seemed it was again
Unter den Linden
Besides die Komische Oper
And Mack the Knife
Cavorting for Jenny
And the black freighter going out to sea
And aboard her
Was me
In an idiot's delight.

I saw Anne Frank Unter den Linden
In a museum for German history

And I alone to contemplate the bronze
For who is there to care
Unter den Linden
Where legs goosestep their terror
Through my heart
Beneath the Yellow Stars.

Humboldt University sits astride
Unter den Linden
The same von Humboldt of my childhood park
Chicago
Where I dreamed idyllic dreams
And attended Talmud Torah
Beside von Humboldt School
Where Jewish childhood danced.
But never mind.

They offer restitution
To make it good again.
German marks for breathless gas
And ovens bearing symbols of Mercedes
Babies rising to the skies on vapored wings.

Restitution?
Give me back my children
From that black freighter
But speak softly now
To me, Unter den Linden.

May 30, 1986
Berlin

Munich '86

The skies distort
Rains fall surrealist
On the streets of Munich
Forming oblique patterns
Through twisted memories.

The cold is a boiling cold
And thunder a fearsome Thor;
The foam falls swiftly
Flat in the beerhalls of the Munich gods;
The dead are dead.

Where are the faces
The young, intense faces,
Their arms stretched fiercely,
Stiffly in fealty to death?

On Odeans Platz
One still listens
To the voices of madness
Even in a Munich storm
Where the skies shake
Of oaths once heard, here:
The overman forever.

I seek the faces of the young
The intense, the eager ones
Who pledged to die
And died among the many
The very many, many

In a surrealism of death
Proving nothing
Absolutely nothing
But that evil is its own reward.

★ ★ ★

To the Munich opera
And in searing accident
I am taken to the box in replication
Where the new gods primped and bowed
To place their shallow imprint
On forever:
Twelve convulsive years
Of a thousand year reich.

A box for kings
And now the new imperium
That was old and gone before inception;
A box reserved for kings
And then for madness:
No eyes turned to me
Euphoric at the opera
It hardly mattered
Nor do they now,
So soon my sorrow.

June 5, 1986
Munich and Lyon

TWO POEMS FROM THE BELLECOUR . . .

Morning on the Bellecour

The Wars of Slogan

On the monument of the children
Is graffiti, at Izieu
The swastika of collaboration
The war of slogan that precedes
The bomb
That always precedes the bomb
While on the Bellecour, Lyon
Horses race a pleasant Sunday morning
Bareback, on heavy track
To cushion injury on the Plaza Bellecour
Where Gestapo bullets
Punctured heads of Frenchmen
Who defied and are forgotten
As martyrdom is always forgotten.

I have seen the Barbie
In his cage of glass
A sallow-faced innocent
Not he would harm a child
Tender is his glance to camera
For after all, he placed roses
On the grave of Jean Moulin
Earning points for kindness in Lyon.

To Hotel Terminus at the Perrach
No longer headquarters of SS

No longer cries of torment
Fill the night of Terminus
Where Barbie wore another face
Not kindly, nor loving of a child
A face of steel
Of terror in the night, or day
Or in between.

I walked the hall of Terminus
Which of sixty doors was his
Which, the torture rooms
Which the rooms where betrayal
Had its glory hours?
Informing Barbie, the elegance
Of France died
As France died.

Swastikas still scratch terror
In the lift of Terminus
But in the lobby a violin is heard:
Meditations from Thais
Meditations of millenia
Will never comprehend
The incomprehensible.

To Saint Joseph Prison
A block or so away
Where Barbie contemplates
His cell
The French tricolors flutter in the wind

While across the street
A new graffiti insists: "Israel Vivra!"
Covering graffiti hating Jews
Hating Jews, of course!

The wars of slogan
Are never-ending
Where are the bombs now pointing?
They point at thee
And me
And at the shallowness of eternity.

May 17, 1987
Lyon, France

Afternoon on the Bellecour

The Informers

White horses and plumed men
Carried banners of the kings
And the races were exquisite
Under the Lyonais sky
On a Sunday afternoon on the Bellecour
Where once there was madness.

Nearby, the Saone and the Rhone
Flow their placid ways to sea
Unhurried, unbloodied now.

I have come
Not to walk the markets of Lyon
Past stalls of produce
From the world
Sweet the tangerines may be
And the berries an enthrallment
In the markets of Lyon.

I have come
Not to prowl for trinkets
Nor for beads
Not to hail Mary in the cathedral
On the hill
Nor scan the Roman ruins nearby,
Munching the fragrant, crispy bread
Of France under a pleasant sun
As now they do.

I seek them, the informers

Who informed
Their ages and their eyes betray
Between the Saone and the Rhone
As they betrayed.

When is the time to revive
A lost war
The Gestapo war
When power was death
To a baby's smile?

Achtung! It was no war
When five by five
The children marched to gas
Singing songs for France
And freedom.

It was no war
For mothers stripped of honor
Naked, on a terror floor
Where fathers, humiliated by evil,
Shamed, unable to protect a child
In time distinctive of all time.

This evil, they informed
The informers

In Lyon their ages, their eyes betray
As they betrayed
Here, between the Saone and the Rhone
In shadows of a cathedral
That could not see
While France convulsed.

May 28 and 29, 1987
Des Artistes, Lyon
Tuileries, Paris

The Testing of Passions

I gave up of the Sabbath
To attend the passions of Mila
The handsome Filipina poet
Imprisoned to a terror state
Now free
And I waited for her passions
How I waited for her passions!

Passions must be there in the recitement of terror
To tell in open verse
Of forgotten dungeons
On Mindanao, or Manila
No matter.

Her verbal rhythms
Told of no death walks on Bataan
No memories of these things
Hovered over her remembrances
Nor do I hear the countercries
Of Balalaika
Soothing steel memories of other imprisonments
Attended by the KGB
As example in a far-forgotten Ural cave.

Close your eyes, Mila
Close your eyes
Perhaps you'll see the terrorized
Unremembered by the dilettantes
Of amnesty

Whose damnesty is now directed
To shame the survivors of Babi Yar, again.

(Oh the monument at Babi Yar
Is still too shallow, too fragile
To rehabilitate our dead, Yevtushenko,
Lest you forget to still remember.)

In your fragment passions, Mila
Gloss away pogrom -- waiting,
Waiting for the budding targets
There are always budding targets
   for these passions
Pamyat, amnesty for the Kluxer killers
Festering in the seams of the Ukraine
Or Crimea
Or Riga, or Bucharest, or Zagreb
North of Jasenovac.

Oh, the Ustasha deserves
Its own cantation
Let us pray in amnesty, for we are civilized
And gentility hovers now over these things past.

In silent passions are amnesties reserved
For the sorrowing
While in the Argentine, mothers
Still seek their disappeared
In tears.

Where are the forgotten children

Of Armenia
Or the Romani
The gentle, songful children of the Romani
Stripped of decencies
And memories
Without a PEN to cry their name
Their shame, in vain.

The history of government
Is often terror loosed by government
Quixote was facade
And chivalries were fraud:
Tell me of the passions slain at Ma'alot
The schoolgirls at Ma'alot
Without an amnesty to scream;
Tell me of the athletes of Judea shattered
At the Munich Olympiad
Are they returned by PEN to Valhalla?
Do mothers sob their losses to PLO slaughter
Passionless?

I gave up of the Sabbath
To listen to the passions of Mila
The handsome poet out of Filipina prison
In Manila.
Her songs contained mere hints of what men do
In finite sorrows

Her songs were not enough
In time they'll hardly matter.
There are too many passions
And often songs are brass and far away
So far away.

Sept. 27, 1991
On the Rubio

Lost Chances

In Sarajevo
Where skis slalom
Their Olympian memories
And skaters will forever race
The frozen lakes
Reliving lost chances
Between bombs.

In Sarajevo
Where 19 year old Javrilo Princip
Pointed pistol at an archduke, crying:
"For Serbian freedom!"
And a world enmeshed darkness
Discovering trenches, poison gas
And lost chances by the millions.

Where German defeat
Festered a twisted cross
And a new order
And new terrors named Ustasha
New gases, new rockets, new atoms
And more lost chances
Than humankind can fathom.

In Sarajevo
At the bus stop
Where we waited for hours
Freezing in the new winter
Of Sarajevo
Her eyes glistened discovery

A student in the faculty of literature
That I, poet of my winter years,
Would be at her side
To Dubrovnik
The medieval castle city
On the Adriatic.

We spoke of books and legends
(Every people must weave its legends)
And rhythms
And song:
The poet must celebrate life
The other will be soon enough coming.

Suddenly it was Dubrovnik
Her eyes searched mine
And I, chilled of my winter years,
Found another lost chance
Rooted in Sarajevo
Which I dare not take.

Nov. 20, 1985
Dubrovnik

The Unmourned

When the horn blows
In its season
Stirring gone memories to life
And the tomorrows of our solemnitudes
Seek out the unremembered shadows
No longer mourned
Long, long unmourned
Who trod the pathways
Of our yesterdays ago
For them the horn blows, too
In the days of our awe.

As a soft wind must bend
A blade of grass or carry
A butterfly away, away
To the sun
The horn blows a celestial cry within
A searing sound of trumpet
Carved from the curved bone of ram
To chill the heart of memory
Of gone yesterdays and impending tomorrows
Across the many lands.

The power of the blast
The fearsome tenderness its cry
Mountains bow in fright

Or dance away in silences of night
Or in the shadowy deeps
Reminding man that forever is not.

Only the horn, as it blows
Can recall the unmourned
Of the yesterdays ago
Or the tomorrows that will in time be lost
For us all.

Jan. 1, 1993
On the Rubio

Poet to Poet

Poet to poet, Ilya:
Where they denied the very Kaddish
To our people: *Zhid,* they cried
And terror ran pogrom on Russian soil
The Cossack and the whip, the knife of terror
The early *pamyat* which we fled
Long yesterdays ago.

Then, commissars decreed that Psalms
May not be sung on Russian soil
And prayers were long, long lost
Forgotten memories of faith
Recalling Jerusalem
Amidst the roars of the bitterness we faced
From czar to commissar.

Ilya Krichevsky conjured a higher song
To defend his nation on stones
Of the Square of Free Russia
In a land of overtones of Babi Yar
And German fists
Where ugliness of *pamyat* is heard
Again, through forests of the land.

Ilya Krichevsky
Poet Krichevsky sang:
"You will not die the way you want to die"
For that is easy
As heroism is not.
And unarmed Ilya Krichevsky climbed alone
Atop a tank equipped for fury

And opened a hatch offering peace
To take a bullet in the head
And die first in defense
Of his new Russia

"Yisgadal, v'yiskadash . . ."
The rabbi chanted the Kaddish heard
Around the world
That our young Russian poet had given his life
Forever
And the president said:
"Sleep peacefully, O heroes!
Let the soil of Russia be feathers for you."

Ilya Krichevsky declaimed his martyrdom
In Jewish sorrows.
There were no cries of *Zhid* that day.

August 25, 1991
On the Rubio

Over Hong Kong Waters

Quiet hovers heavy over Hong Kong waters
Ships roost, awaiting turns at drydock
While overhead clouds gather
To spread thunder across this bay
Engulfing mammoth ships
Then relenting
And all of us remembering
Who is really lord of the sea:
Iron or storm?

Our last night in port
Only few on deck to notice
The hydrofoil skimming waters to Macau
A junk here or there without sail
Petrol-powered now, pulling nets
For the fishpots of China
The bay polluted with waste
Of a thousand ships roosting
Awaiting turns at drydock
To receive coats of paint and grease
The cosmetics for the sea.

The ship's crew on binge ashore
Crowd Tsim Sha Tsui
And its tinsel: some for the foods
They'll not find in the galley
On the morrow
Some to relearn the ways of spirits
Or sample, for a time, procreation

In some noxious bar, for Hong Kong dollars
The open sesame for men who sail
The shrinking seas of loneliness.

I walk the decks of the container ship
In the gathering dusk
Beneath another dark cloud over Hong Kong waters
The roosting ships disappearing in the night
A warm wind sweeps
From the south across the bay
A wind that will embrace us
Or batter us on our way
When the sun comes up again like fire
Over Hong Kong Bay.

May 6, 1988
Hong Kong Bay

Chantey of Harry Prigg at Sea

Down the damn curtains
In my little flat
Get ready for me
Get ready for me
The sun's broken through
The sea's running fast
Get ready, get ready for me.

The sea, she's no mistress
Her waves are too cold
Her spray strikes like ice-fired sand
Fluff the damn pillows
And spray thee Arpege
The sea's running fast by command.

Down those damn curtains
There's no time to tarry
I come thee a long lonesome way
Fluff the damn pillows
Fluff them with song
Fluff them
Oh I'll be along!

May 21, 1988
South China Sea

When We Are Told

When we are told
And inward castles fall away
Before our time
In frightful suddenness
As reality grabs the throat
Which cannot scream
Which may not scream
As tomorrows move away
Remorselessly, swiftly
Without warning they move away
When we are told . . .

Take my hand as I take yours
We are the tested ones
Contesting the Big C
The ominous biggest of Cs,
Contesting for time
To hear the laughter of a child
To face the morning sun
On its spatial trek across the firmament

Or to stare again in awe
Wondrous awe
Upon a nightly sapphired sky
And sigh . . .

These are our tomorrows
They whirl about in beauty

Through the hot summer days
Or breathless through the crisp wintry winds.

We'll have them yet in full abundance
Many tomorrows
If we will it as we must
Or all is lost.

Dec. 7. 1988
On the Rubio

Secrets

A castle at Brandeis
Bathed in warm spring rain
Pathways at Brandeis
Where my son walked to class
Or sold his sandwiches
To make it cum laude.

Here were his secrets
Which a father may not pry
The students, the sorrows
The dreams I could not share
Nor would I share
For each is a lonely life
Not to intrude nor be tampered.

Mine, he'll never know
The transplant of dreams
They never work, nor should they
But once I dreamed for the better world
It came stark, hollow, abused
It came computerized and often bitter
But on a wayward path
I came upon a flower or two
That pleased.

Tomorrow, next week or the next
There will be birth
As it must for the species
And one day my son will reflect

Secrets withheld, unshared
By his child — as they must.

For his, as mine and thine
Is a lonely life
Not to intrude nor tamper
Even on pathways at Brandeis
Of a warm, spring rain
Beside a castle of learning.

June 20, 1986
Brandeis University
Waltham, Mass.

The Hebrew Melody

Robert returned
My brother of gentle soul
The son of Solomon
Came back to me while the fiddler
The Russian fiddler now free
Played a Hebrew melody
A thin line of subdued sorrow
In the minor scales
Heartbreak is always of the minor scales.

The Hebrew melody, its slow
Undulating waves of song
Struck the shores of my remembrance
A melody my brother used to play
The one he learned from the music teacher
Down the block
Who traded half an hour
Of patience
For his fifty cents
A lesson for my brother
A tender Hebrew melody
For my big brother who learned so well
As I watched
Alas, there was not another
Fifty cents for me.

My head was turned by the melody
The Hebrew melody
In the minor key
That washed against my heart

And I sat entranced
On the window ledge
To watch my brother play
His bowing corrected by the teacher
Many times corrected
But does it matter?

Three score years ago and more
The melody leaped across the chasms
Of my memories
In the magic tones of a fiddler
Now free
Who understood the melancholies of a song
A Hebrew song in minor key
And I heard it all again
The thin soft lines of sorrow
That remind me
Yesterdays are forever gone

Ai-eee!
Ai-eee!

Aug. 6, 1989
On the Rubio

Who is Wise?

Who is wise and who is honored?
He who takes a gentle bride
She who shares his towering dreams
They are wise and they are honored.

Who is wise and who is honored?
He who treasures tenderness
She whose eyes are jeweled stars
They are wise and they are honored.

Who is wise and who is honored?
My son, my son's idyllic vision
His bride, his bride above all rubies
They are wise and they are honored.

Who is wise and who is honored?
He who dreams of fatherhood
She who sighs for motherhood
They are wise and they honored.

Theirs is love among the honored
Theirs is love beyond the far stars
Send them warm and gentle winds
For they are wise and I am honored.

March 21, 1991
On the Rubio

My Father, My Hero

My father was no hero
In the war against Japan.

Soldiers, if they live to tell it
Become story-tellers
About the wars against Japan
Or the Kaiser
Or the German (there is a difference!)

My father was no hero
In his war against Japan:
A baker to the Czar
He killed no one
Except, perhaps
With the qualities of Russian bread.

But there was an insistency
About my father, my hero
That one points no weapons
For a government of pogrom
Even against Japan,
An insistency that one must flee:
"Go West, young man, go West!"
To Ellis Island? To Galveston?
To the Yukon?
The tales he'd weave about the Yukon
He was not to see
And he left the Brazos River
In Texas, to me
Later, later

For my own war against Japan
A story-teller too, and not a hero
Not a hero, indeed.

Like father
Like son.

To Chicago, the city by the sea
Oh the legacy he left, there
For me
And the stories he told
And his dreams would enchant my dreams
With their many splendored possibilities.

Each night, Peter Rabbit and I
Or was it time for Tom Sawyer and Huck
Or the Zionist dreams of Theodor Herzl?
Never mind. All were tucked away
By my father, my hero
Who told his stories to me
Only to me.

They told of loftier forms of heroics
By my father, the sorcerer of ideas
And possibilities
Who promised me that life would be
  measured
By insightful men and women
Who stalked the earth
Seeking beauty, touching stars.

And he said to me :
There would be time for singing
And there would be time for song.

Herb Brin
Chicago and the
Rubio
July 2 and 3, 1994

In Lamentation

A young Jewish woman leaves her home in Holland and is taken to a nazi detention camp at Westerbork during a dark moment in 1942. Her journey ends in Poland.

Torn by the events, her husband attempts to express his grief in lamentation. The unsigned expression of grief and loneliness was found somewhere in the Netherlands after the war and printed in Dutch newspapers.

The husband's identity was never known, but his anguish for his beloved wife touched the heart of a nation. The lamentation was translated roughly into English by Felix and Flory Van Beek of Newport Beach, themselves survivors of the tragedy.

They asked Herb Brin to add cadence to the love story.

Loneliness

Your lips
Which I have kissed so much
Your hair
So dark and tousled
Your heart
Your young and tender heart
On which I rested my head
In gentle, loving passion.

Did it have to be this way
I asked within

For I do not know whether you died
How and when — so far away.

Are you in pain
Are you in hunger
What wanderings are left to us
Before we are together
Again?

That early spring morning
When you left our home
Wearing your white, thin blouse
How sunny and happy you were
For neither of us heard
The soft rustlings of death
Neither of us could see
The scepter of fate
The shadowy wings of forever
Flying over your face
That turned to me
Radiantly smiling
Then.

During all those fearsome nights
And days
It seemed I detected your brisk
Light steps
Walking our stairs
And then, nothing but a single letter
A dreaded form letter

Bearing your name, a stamp of Germany
The barrack number that became your home
And you asked for warm clothing.

My heart refused to break
Just then
Oh not just then
For I saw you somewhere very far
Alone
Standing near a river
Was it beside the waters of Babylon
Wearing a slave's chain?

□ *The author takes up the memories of youth:*

If I had Aladdin's wonderlamp
And the flying carpets of the sultans
And the caliphs
I would fly the clouds of memory
Until I might descend upon your camp
My arms to embrace you tightly
Never again to let you go
But to lift you to the skies
And the stars
To the islands of Epipsychidion, Orpheus or Ogygia
To long forgotten shores
There to be together, my Calypso,
To kiss your hands
Which tended our home so lovingly
And then
And then, kiss your dark and tousled hair.

Who knows whether we will see each other
Again
Is there but one purpose to the tortures
To our severed threads of life
That were woven for a shattered fragment
Of forever?

But then
To live without a shadow of hope
Is not enough
And so we cling in dream, my beloved,
You and I
To the dream that we shall return
To our paradise
The one given to me when I had you
Where the winds of love were soft and playful
Exotic beneath exquisite trees
Where you, whom I loved so deeply,
Shall again caress my tired head.

Our last kiss was swift
Too swift, too short
As farewells slipped away
In the union of our lips
Quickly, with a smile
So very quickly.

My heart aches for you
As I must ask:
How will that final kiss
Survive eternity?

On the Rubio
March 10, 1994

In Epilogue

Jack Pressman, rabbi emeritus of Temple Beth Am in Los Angeles, a respected poet on the American scene, composed the following assessment of the work of Herb Brin.

To the Bard of the Rubio

You view the tree, the rill, the sea.
The tragic comedy of everyday.
And hug, or weep, or sigh.
But never yawn and turn away.

You put off ill-fitting trappings
Of a society of values false or empty.
You set aside imprisoning shoes
And step into the rover's sandals
Which must be shined or else called "shabby"
And doff the "clothes that make the man"
And wrap your battered "Nahvi"
And grasp the gnarled Moses staff
And climb out of the Rubio.

The wide world has become your home.
You've taken to your heart as kin
The color, size, belief, or bent
Which comes with woman and with man.
Your diary begins with Adam
And overflows with unborn tomorrows.
You thrill to every glint of beauty
Expand with pride at every miracle
Performed for, by or to your people
You rage
At every tragic inhumanity,

At every murder of the seed of Abel
By the seed of Cain the Marked
Wherever, whenever; and you weep
For Samson, Absalom, Uriah and Akiba,
Crusaders' victims and Conversos,
The ashes of York's Tower, *Auto-da-Fe,*
Of Babi Yar and Birkenau.

You are moved to poetry
By human pain or glory.
How shall we call you?
Names like publisher, reporter,
Editor or essayist fall too short
Of definition of your calling.
The crowds by puffery beguiled
May fail to recognize your persona and your gift,
Because your lack of self-aggrandizement
Permits the beaters of the drums and chests
To seem to be what you in truth have been.

But let them rant.
Your words, your aptly chosen words,
Spare phrases, ripe with imagery,
Intangibles rich with spirit and hue.
Timeless and boundless.
Your words possess a life that is their own
In the souls of the discerning and the feeling.
And the lovers who would wrap their arms
Around the whole aching world
And kiss it to take the pain away and make it better
Your words will resonate
Because

It is your words alone which can define you.
They rustle in the trees of your wadi
So buffeted and blessed at nature's whim,
And whisper, "Here lives the Bard of Rubio."

Jacob Pressman
April, 1994

YESTERDAY'S GARDEN

□

A sampler of previously published Poems by Herb Brin

Song

The land is barren, free of grace
Without a song to sing its ways . . .

Tell me the songs your people sing
And I shall assess your time
Tell me your chants and Iliads
And I shall mark your day.

Within the song lie passions of an age:
Enchantments of man's tenderness, or rage.

I implore my land:
Learn the art of song,
The wonderment of line
The melodies of time.

Charge

I charge you with a wondrous ear
My song on a seeking ear
To scan my art with a wondrous eye
And should you not — well, then

I charge you with a searching ear
To hear with me the magic sea
Or the wind on an unseen hill
Or a falling leaf upon the grass
Or a star beyond the glass.

I charge you with a reaching eye

To scan a flower on desert air
And gasp at a spectrum of afterrain
Or stumble dismay or ecstasy
In grass of forbidden fields.

My lines I press upon your brow
Come, hear them now
Come hear them now.

May 12, 1964
San Diego
From: *Wild Flowers*

A Song of Magic

A child with a tear
Sheds a torment for me
His grief tears the heavens apart

Oh I'd bring him a song
To soften his wrong
And a trick
And a trick for a start

For the trace of a smile
I'd tumble a mile
I'd tangle the trees
For a child

And weave for him tales
Of high-flying whales
Of princes
Of kingdoms beguiled

Oh I'd sing him of places
Where monkeys make faces
At rhinos that frolic on air
And I'd pop a balloon
For my friend the baboon
And I'd dance with a laughing bear

A sob and a fear
Would soon disappear
And he'd laugh
At a tipsy giraffe

Or a turtle that sings
Of wondrous things
Or a lion on butterfly wings

Oh child of my heart
Oh child of my heart
Grief tears the heavens apart.

Dec. 7, 1965
In flight to L.A.
From: *Justice, Justice*

Children of Brown

Do they sing, these children.
Of Alice Blue gown.
These children of fear
And ghettos of brown?

Does a sandman come
As their sun goes down
Bringing sweet slumber
For children of brown?

Do they pray to awake
In a magical town
of daffodil dreams
On pillows of down?

Do they dance in the meadow
Or laugh at a clown
That tumbles for joy
For the children of brown?

Does a God in his heaven
Carry a frown
To watch what men do
To the children of brown?

Aug. 10, 1966
Chicago
From: *Justice, Justice*

Free

— to Harry Lang

My blood soaks deep
Where Russian passions sleep.

The *shtetl* and the sigh
The *pilpul* and the cry
"Pogrom!"
Against a tremble sky.

Their Christ is risen
In their tortured land
Where I must flee
Or die their death
Bedamned.

The fist that held their sickle
Harvested my blood
In Russian mud.

From this I fled
Book in hand
Prayer overhead
To seek another land
Untroubled bed.

Steerage was my lot
And strange my ancient tongue
My ways misunderstood
Of thee, of thee I sung!

Oh I have seen the Lady
Raise her lamp
Upon my storm-tossed sea

Thrusting light through night
For me.

For me?

And in a searing flash
I was, they said, now free.

But also free
To walk a city's street
For bread
To peddle laces in the sleet
For bed.

But free
To stalk the halls of learning
In the night
To stand as man,
To question — or to fight.

No crown of thorn
They'll press upon my brow
I walk a picket line
Or milk a cow
I watch a sea gull on a silver wing
And if I choose
I fashion song, and sing.

Malibu
Jan. 29, 1968
From *Conflicts*

Two Signs

Honest Arnie, he's a card
His sign is a saucy line:
"Another Load of Used Cows!"
His wheels are hot
The shackles hard
Meat on the hoof
From farm to yard
And the steers — without tears.

The truck is a money load
On Arnie's endless road
To hook and case
To pan and flame.

Where there's no tear
There's no shame.

The driver smiled to pass me by
The sign was long
The sign was high
His load of cows
To broil or fry.

But then a black-faced steer and I
Stared fleetingly, eye to eye
I knew a life was soon to die.

And what am I?
Oh what am I?

Another day, another place
The steer perhaps was human face

A child upon another course
A world sees, without remorse
A cattle car, a cattle train
A child without a name:

Cry my child,
Your world's wild.

Oh Honest Arnie, he's a card
At least is sign is a saucy line.

At Auschwitz man found other fun
In German mirth (In German gun!)
In iron letters terror high:
"*Arbeit Macht Frei*"
One laughs, one laughs — to die.

Who is animal,
What am I?

August 8, 1965
On the Santa Ana Freeway
From: *Justice, Justice*

Song For Odette

There was the time in occupied France when a powerful nation hunted down Jewish children. One was Odette.

I cup my hands
I blow dandelions to the wind
Oh, a tender-touching wind
That fans the face
Like wisps of eyelid upon the cheek
A butterfly kiss.

And away, away they fly
Puffs of dandelion to the sky
High
To the sun
And try as I sigh to shade
The eye
My vision blurs.

Odette
For you this happy song
Of sunshine and dandelion
And a fleckless sky
And Alpine waters tracing
Rivulets
To a child's Riviera of dream.

I must not tell
I must not tell
To take the magic
From this happy song

And blur my eyes with fires
Of memory.

For eyes burn
And tears reveal a hunted child
Oh, hunted, hunted, hunted
Child.

Where to hide the night
Where to hide the day
Where to hide the end of false papers
And false names
And real hungers
And imagined beauties?

Are there not beauties
In the fields of France
Even the German France?

Find a magic meadow
There must be one
I have it on faith there must be one
And gather you dandelions
In your cupped hands
And if the wind forsakes
Blow them with your breath
And they will fly away
And they will fly away
Gossamer to the innocence
Of sky
High, to the sun.

Sing, Odette
Sing, Odette
And run!

Jan. 1, 1981
Los Angeles
From: *Justice, Justice*

The Cobbler

"May no evil eye befall thee,"
And the cobbler with a sigh
His eyes went leaping through me
Deeply seeping, weeping through me
Until I felt to die.

Hunched, he was
A trunk of man
Bent by the lines
That coursed his brow
Saying:
(Oh — hear it now!)

"Sons as strong as the forest tree
Eyes as clear as they ought to be
Blue as the rolling northern sea
These sons were mine
And they were three . . ."

The cobbler's bench had here and there
A shoe, a shoe for his repair
And who can stitch a man's despair
In a cobbler's shop in Tel Aviv
Where darkened corners grieve?

A son, devoted to the law
Testing that which reason saw;
A son for whom excitement stirred
In magic weavings of a word;
And there was one

And there was one . . .
All torn apart
By the German gun.

The cobbler soled my son's worn shoes
A soul with nothing more to lose
Caressing them, consoling me:
"No evil eye upon thee."

Malibu
Oct. 17, 1969
From: *Conflicts*

The Dream of Ali Gaby

Hussein Ali Gaby
My guide, my friend
May you find a wife
Dazzling tight in American pants
Glittered, bejeweled
A cinemaed dream
Bedded at your side
Pillowed deep in television's suburbia
An Aladdin lamp nearby
To bring you magic
Of the years to come
For you are young
And your dreams are fragment many.

But take me to your tents
Hussein Ali Gaby
Where they dance the ancient belly sands
Of Egypt
Across a sluggish Nile
Where debris flows
Through cavem cities of hunger
Where tourists flock
From Europe, from America
To "give a look."
No matter.

Dazzle me, Hussein Ali Gaby
With the waving veils
And the heaving breasts
Encrusted with glitter

Of glass
And the undulating intrigue
Beyond the pyramids and fluttering arms
Where ecstatic sounds drift
Sensuous swift beyond the sands
Only to die
Against hovels of your homes
Nearby
That slum the ancient sandscape
And the towering stones
Amidst a jungle of baksheesh
And camel dung
For a loaf of bread.

I found no reeds along your Nile
No Pharaoh's daughter
Pulling her basket of Moses
To these shores
Nor my people here
Long, long, gone.

Tut's jewels are lifeless
Encased in glass
Priceless, worthless fossils
They buy no American wife
For Hussein Ali Gaby
My guide, my friend
Whose tour car to the Sphinx
Or to the dance
Is a fragile ticket
To a cinema dream
One day

One day to be bedded at his side.

Hussein Ali Gaby
My guide, my friend
May you dream so long.

Feb. 24, 1981
At the Sphinx, Cairo
From: *My Spanish Years*

The Day Man Walked the Moon

Considerations of jailed Joseph Maizlish, history major who challenged the wars and consciences of man . . .

The moon is far
Beyond Joe's iron bar
Contorted
Seen through iron screen

For them it's go
Joe
Wouldn't you know
All the way from Kokomo
(Like they'd say in vau-de-vo!)
And the count's quite clear
For any Joe who'll hear.

For them, or you
It's go, go, go
On charcoaled cheese
Explored in rocketry — and ease
Or down below
Where crescent moonbeams blast
Your hell
Clapped beyond your far-forgotten cell
I know, I know
Joe.

What, indeed, are vistas of the wild?
A trick that's played

In some far distant place
The bouncing of a man
On sunburst rock
Across uncharted space
When none alive can stop his clock
Not hide his face.
From power, nor disgrace
Where madmen dwell
Who shoot to kill
Beyond your cell
The day men walked the moon.

To walk a speck of dust
Because it's there
(And someone must, I trust)
Beyond the reach of air
Or thrust a rocket to a star
Or sock it to the sun
From where you are
Held by gun.

They plant no flags to conscience
Nor acclaim
Him who probes frontiers
Of human shame.

They beat no paths to reason
Where you dwell
Captive of their bars
That steel your name
In some bleak agony of hell
Where blood's their futile game

And government's aflame.

But then, I know that some must walk
Automaton
Or men, bouncing high
On cages of their moons
While some must scan the ravages within
Clapped in silence of an iron cell.

Who can measure
What the cosmic mind must do?
Where is reason, where is man's frontier?

Computered souls
They leap in loneliness
And then there's Joe
And then, there's always Joe.

Chicago
July 22, 1969
From *Conflicts*

The Bon Homme Richard

Bands played
Like rat-a-tat-tat
When the Bon Homme Richard
Came to town
Town
Old Diego Town
With flare and with blare
Like blow the men down
And a hi-diddle-diddle olé
And a hi-diddle-diddle
Olé?

Boom, boom
No tears and no gloom
In old Diego Town this day.

Oh say can you see
Empty hangars on me
The Bon Homme Richard home from sea
The Bon Homme Richard
Home from sea?

Flag-draped
Are the crates below deck
And the blue runneth yonder
Of blood
And screams sing distortions of song
Distortions of song that went wrong.

Like toot-toot

Like root-a-toot-toot
And the joys of reunion
On deck
What the heck
Korea's a speck far away
Korea's a speck far away?

Pink lemonade
And a laughter parade
And flags fill the air
Everywhere
Where pilots once bled
Now speeches are said
And brass hides the sounds of foray
And brass hides the sounds of foray?
Hip, hooray!

Years passed
In old Diego Town
Or was it a day
Or a frown?
Time plays a helluva game
And man is a lousy clown
And man is a lousy clown.

But, boom-boom
In old Diego Town
The Bon Homme Richard's come to town
Town
Old Diego Town
With flare and with blare
Once again

With flare and with blare once again?

Like toot-toot
Like root-a-toot-toot
And the joys of reunion on deck
What the heck
Hanoi's a speck far away
Hanoi's a speck far away!

Flag-draped
Are the crates below deck
And the blue runneth yonder
Of blood
And screams sing distortions of song
Distortions of song that go wrong.

Time plays
A helluva game
And life's a recurring trip
Like root-toot
Like root-a-toot-toot
You never give up the ship
Boys
You never give up the ship.

San Diego and Malibu
Sept. 3, 1967
From: *Conflicts*

I Invented Time

Hold back your clocks
Damn it, no requiem for me!
I'll rust those gears
With the fire spray of seas
That sweep my autumn years.

Crusts of age clog my knees
But I'll get along
At a lesser pace
At a lesser pace.

And softer my sighs
Gentler, more gentle
And as suns descend
I'll get along
It's moonlight saving time
For me.

I've many a mountain yet to climb
And the hot breath of lips on mine
And the touch of tender hips.

Are there promises to keep?
Don't count my ways
Don't count my ways.

The brook, the stream, the massive sea
Hold many mysteries for me
And books unread
And paths untrod

Primeval forests beckon me.

Don't speed my way to dreams undreamed
I've cantatas to create
I've heady lilacs yet to sense
And little foxes to divine.

Take back your clocks
Hold back your clocks
With searing breath of lips
On mine
I invented time.

April 28, 1982
London
From: *My Spanish Years*

POEMS from the RUBIO

OTHER BOOKS BY HERB BRIN

POETRY

Wild Flowers

Justice, Justice

Conflicts

My Spanish Years

OVERSEAS STUDIES

Ich Bin Ein Jude
— A search for roots of
evil in Europe

Where are the Children?
— Raising a mirror to German
leadership, demanding answers.